for Jeanette,
with all arm ?

The Collective

Nouns

For Birds

by

Amanda

Huggins

Amanda Huggins

Maytree Press 2020

Published 2020 by Maytree Press

www.maytreepress.co.uk

ISBN: 978-1-9135080-0-5

A CIP catalogue record of this book is available from the British Library.

Cover image: The Charm © Alice Parker

Maytree 011

Printed in the UK by PiggyPrint

For Claudia

Contents

Acknowledgements

A previous version of *The New Knowing*, titled *Northern Light*, formed part of the Northern Poetry Society's Poem of the North in 2018. *The Weight of Everything* first appeared in Poems for the NHS (Onslaught Press) 2018. *Cows* first appeared in Words for the Wild anthology 2018. *Out Chasing Boys* was shortlisted for The Walter Swan Poetry Prize 2018. *All I Can Show You* was shortlisted for The Walter Swan Poetry Prize 2018. *Dizzy With It* was shortlisted for the Hysteria Prize 2016 and was first published in the Hysteria anthology 2016, and in Reflections, the Cleckheaton Literature Festival anthology, in 2018. *At The Kitchen Table* first appeared in The Cotton Grass Appreciation Society anthology (Maytree Press) 2019. *The Names of Seaweed and Collective Nouns for Birds* was longlisted for the Fish Poetry Prize in 2019. A flash fiction version of *Listing* was published on the Spelk website in 2019.

About the Author

Amanda Huggins is the author of the flash fiction collection, *Brightly Coloured Horses*, and the short story collection, *Separated From the Sea*, which received a Special Mention in the 2019 Saboteur Awards. Her second full-length collection, *Scratched Enamel Heart*, published May 2020, features her prize-winning story from the 2018 Costa Short Story Award.

She has been placed and listed in numerous fiction and poetry competitions including Fish, Bridport, Bath, InkTears, the Alpine Fellowship Writing Award and the Colm Toibin International Short Story Award. Her travel writing has also won several awards, notably the BGTW New Travel Writer of the Year in 2014, and she has twice been a finalist in the Bradt Guides New Travel Writer Award.

Amanda grew up on the North Yorkshire coast, moved to London in the 1990s, and now lives in West Yorkshire.

Out Chasing Boys

We spent summer on the seafront,
two stranded mermaids
killing time.
We rolled up our jeans,
carried our shoes,
blew kisses at the camera
in the photo booth.
Always out, chasing boys,
as if we had forever.

In the clamour and haze
of O'Reilly's arcade,
we revered those rake-limbed lads
on the slot machines
as though they were gods,
not fishermen's lads.
And our laughter cascaded
over penny falls,
as we pouted, hands on hips,
all flirt and glance,
eyes half-closed with the want
of something we didn't understand.

The New Knowing

We sit side by side on the playground swings
and talk of the shine in a distant city.
Two homespun girls turned restless moths,
dancing around these northern lights,
cleaved by hope to this one-trick town
that keeps hearts and wings from heading south.

Yet there's a softness to the air tonight,
as though we've made it somewhere else —
a place more gentle, where boys whisper in Italian,
and the put-put of scooters can be heard
on a distant coastal road.

Then everything falls silent, and we know,
know for one brief moment of teenage clarity,
that life will be good and worth the wait.
We each hold the new knowing close to our ribs
and don't speak of it, just in case it isn't true.

The Names of Seaweed and Collective Nouns for Birds

When I saw Da's salt-licked boots,
frayed cap tossed over the peg,
I'd throw down my satchel,
punch the stiff latch
and crash through the scullery,
knowing he'd be
hauling coal from the cellar,
cheeks smudged with black dust,
strangely clumsy out of water.

The tug of the tide left him breathless
when he stayed too long on the shore,
and he lived among us only half-listening
to our land-locked talk,
always waiting to set sail again.

Sea child, he called me,
his slip of a fish,
as we dived down deep
to the coral beds
where mermaids sang
and jellyfish danced in puffball skirts.

Mam hoped he would turn his back on the tiller,
be coaxed ashore to the herring sheds,
be anchored down by kipper and creel.
Yet Da would never trade his fins for feet.

And when I lie awake on summer nights,
the last of the light
holding out in the western sky,
I hear him recite the names of seaweed
and collective nouns for birds.

In dreams I'm deafened
by a clamour of purple claw,
lured by a charm of oyster thief,
double-crossed by a deceit of devil's tongue,
chased by a scold of landlady's wig,
outwitted by a gaggle of dabberlocks.

Then at dawn he slides beneath the waves,
drowning with the names still on his tongue,
leaving me alone once more
to run aground without him.

Dizzy With It

We wrote our songs on Saturdays,
after Chelsea Girl and the Wimpy Bar,
lyrics strewn with doodled stars
scattered across your bedroom floor.

I play-play-played those dented drums—
three cast-off cake tins of your mam's,
accompanied by the pick and strum
of your wreck-necked red guitar.

And we thought we'd go far,
we were dizzy with it.

You taped it all on your dad's reel-to-reel:
my unsure voice, your backing hum,
the dum-dum-thrum
of those battered drums,
and the slip-slide-scratch of six steel strings.

We'd stop and dance to the radio, when
the DJ revealed the week's top ten,
your Bolan curls a half-crazed tangle,
and my patched-up pale-sky jeans
embroidered with all our rockstar dreams.

No Doubt

If I ever question my love for you,
aware that the years have wearied its shine,
knowing we can't outrun
the ravages of familiarity,
then I picture life without you.

I have you stolen by a nameless illness,
some freak accident or fall,
taken without saying goodbye.
I imagine the house
still strewn with your possessions:
that cracked, tea-stained mug I loathe,
your shaving brush left out to dry
with the bristles over-splayed,
a ziggurat of half-read books,
each marked with scribbled notes,
newspaper folded open at the crossword,
waiting for you to solve that final clue.

Not forgetting those four small nails
on the kitchen table,
left there as though to vex me.

I can feel them in my hand,
weightless, featherlight,
yet sharp as loss,
and I know there is no doubt,
no question.
My grief pours out, unstoppable,
until I hear your key in the door.

At the Kitchen Table

The late spring snow
catches us off-guard,
drifts against the henhouse wall,
blots out the distant fells.

And here, in this borrowed house,
we watch, transfixed,
brave the blizzard
to throw scraps for the birds,
half-wishing it could always be like this.

Just you and I
at the kitchen table —
a dog-eared novel,
the weekend papers,
the last bottle of wine
waiting on the shelf
until the sheep are fed.

Yet we know
the snow will thaw by morning,
and we'll drive down the lane
for bread and logs,
ice-melt from the trees
pattering on the bonnet.

Then, too soon,
the workday grind will call us back
from this adopted life
to the small house in the town,
where everything is a little less bright
and a little less kind.

As we leave,
the weather will change again,
the brilliant shine of it
making us smile,
and I'll point out a new-born lamb,
his pink ears backlit by the sun,
as he watches us drive away.

Scars

Life is the shape of all our scars,
these silver threads, gashes, grooves,
the milestones of falls,
reminders of accidents,
or a push too hard
after one too many.

This curved incisor at the base of my thumb,
a tooth made by claw
when the deaf cat was roused from sleep
and turned.

The broken ladder on my outer thigh
from when I ran, eight years old,
across an abandoned site
half-concealed by willow herb,
caught out by a rogue rod
rusting in reinforced concrete.

That dent, a lone dimple in my cheek,
from when I crashed, all temper tantrum,
down the bathroom steps, aged three,
and the deepest dogleg
running north to west behind my ear,
where a flash of anger sliced my skin
and hardened my heart.

This new one is a square of flesh,
incised, removed and cauterized,
the one I call my battle scar,
as I watch it fade with hope.

A Heavy, Haloed Star

As we drove homeward
that dull December evening,
the city lights vanished behind us,
and endless broken lines
stitched motorway lanes in place,
one by one, on and on,
leading us away
from our sometime Eden.
We sang aloud to the radio,
stolen time still carrying us high,
and when our brightness palled,
we turned to the chirp of small talk,
offered mints and bottled water,
not daring to let the car choke up
with silence
when time was running out again.
A heavy, haloed star
hung low in the winter sky,
mistaken, at first, for a plane coming in to land,
and I recalled the Angel of the North
when she first spread her wings
in the year we met.

All I Can Offer

When you carry your grief in front of you,
held high, spilling out like water from
some makeshift vessel,
I cannot lift it from you.
I can only offer the quiet
of the evening as the light fades
and sand martins circle the dunes,
the weight of freckled pebbles
held tight as hope within your palm.
I can only show you the spoils of the tide,
new things wrought from the old:
jewels of clouded sea glass,
gnarled driftwood boughs,
and rounded nubs of pottery
patterned with faded birds,
perhaps teacups once, on an ocean liner,
trembling in their saucers,
crashing to the galley floor
when the wild storm came.

And when we return to the house at dusk,
I can only offer my hand to steady yours,
both of us knowing we are akin to the earth,
always hoping we can somehow stay the same,
wrestling in vain with restless tides,
as the sea demands our endless change.

Frozen Fish

Passing by the lily pond
in that deep December snow,
you glimpsed the goldfish,
a prisoner beneath thin ice.
I cracked the surface with my heel
and we scooped him up with a paper cup,
carried him home in mittened hands,
warmed him with clouds of chocolatey breath.

He spent winter in a borrowed bowl,
and we admired his shimmer,
his glint and gleam,
as he circled the pirate ship,
weaving through weed
in a one-man glittering shoal,
making eyes at the mermaid
with the yellow plait.

In April we carried him back
to the pond in a jar,
squatted at the edge to watch him explore,
saw his tail flick once
before he was gone,
leaving nothing to say he was ever there;
only the echo of a memory
in a single ripple.

Chris Clarke-with-an-e

I see you by the bar at Amy's wedding,
an almost-stranger in your married skin,
much taller than I'd thought you'd be:
my all grown up Chris Clarke-with-an-e.

The boy whose kisses stung my lips
with the tang of sherbet lemons,
sharpening my colours behind the vaulting horse.

'You're my bird for keeps,' the love note said,
scrawled with a cheap dip pen
and smudged where you'd folded it too soon.

Now you call my name as I turn to go,
I feign surprise, blush as we gush our shy hellos
and you say I'm looking well.

Then we both walk away, suddenly unsure,
perhaps kept apart by things unsaid,
half-curious to know our different ending:
grown-up me and Chris Clarke-with-an-e.

The Weight of Everything

The nurse, one hand pressed against her forehead
and the other against the wall,
looked up when she heard my footsteps pass,
smiled briefly, smoothed down her skirt
and turned back to the ward.

Later, at home, when I lay between cool sheets,
I closed my eyes and conjured her face,
understood the weight of everything her smile contained,
wondered if she was still watching over you
in the toss and turn of your hospital bed.

At dawn, I drove past quiet houses, dark, still filled with sleep,
then stopped abruptly at a red light, even though I was alone.
And as I waited I glimpsed a single bright lamp
in an upstairs room,
and hoped it was my nurse, home from her shift.

Voices

Back from the capital and your fancy crowd,
you make shy bogmen of us at Friday supper,
turn us into cloth cap cousins, our voices flat and dull.

Yet Saturday rubs away your strangers' vowels,
swaps something for nothing for owt for nowt,
those southern exclamations for ee by gum,
and by Sunday you're our Yorkshire lad again,
as though you'd never stepped south of Leeds.

Not Quite You

I see you curled in the kitchen chair,
stretched out on the sun-bright ledge,
yet a second glance turns cat to hat—
a conjuring trick reversed.

Sometimes I glimpse you in the yard,
tail winding around the bins,
yet up close, there's a stripe adrift,
an extra smudge of grey beneath the chin,
an amber eye too pale,
a smile too wide, too Cheshire.

Each of these cats are not-quite-you,
a doesn't-pass-muster second best.

None have the tiny heart
that beat against my leg, as faint as a bird's,
as you slept on my lap,
so thin and frail, in your life's last days.
None have the feisty spirit
that flew from beneath your ribcage
as I pressed my hand gently into your fur
in that small, green, sterile room.
So brief a life, so brief a death,
stopped short at that last quiet breath,
yet still your fragile heart beats
some distant rhythm inside my own.

Listing

We were shown to the back of Margot's bistro,
seated at a table listing to the left,
and you folded a ticket from the Pompidou,
tried to wedge the unsteady leg.
Yet everything still slid around
as though we were at sea,
my knife clattering on the tiles,
your napkin fluttering to the floor.

We both said it didn't matter,
our smiles brittle
as we ate overcooked sole
and yesterday's bread,
sipped wine, slightly too acidic,
not properly chilled.

And as the silence deepened,
we drank too much, too fast,
ordered a second carafe,
because it did matter after all.
Turned out we were listing too,
and what would once have made us laugh
had become something else,
to which we never would confess.

I already knew that when we parted at St Pancras
you'd hug me tighter than ever before
and say how lovely it had been,
still waving goodbye as you headed for the Tube.
Yet by Belsize Park you would know
the best way to tell me it was over.

Turn of the Tide

Tow-haired lasses on piebald ponies,
soot-faced, bare-backed,
collecting sea coal in blackened sacks,
their fathers, brothers,
eyes narrowed against outsiders
as they wait for the turn of the tide.

There's those who've tried to erase this village,
pack fishermen off to inland towns
with a suitcase of curl-edged promises,
hoping to hand their cottages to city folk
who paint over the past
with Farrow and Ball.

Yet how could they leave the sea
they breathe,
eyes narrowed against outsiders
as they wait for the turn of the tide.

Sparrows

Glimpsed from the kitchen window,
snarled up in the fence across the field,
a tangle of coal tar feathers,
the flutter of something white,
a wing snagged in the wire.

I pull on heavy boots,
slip your cutters in my pocket,
yet hesitate at the door,
still half-afraid to go.

I recall the sparrows,
their dance across my windscreen,
the dazzle of low sunshine,
music turned up loud on the radio,
the tiny thud
when one of them dipped too low.

There is no sun today,
only this chance for absolution
below a dishwater sky,
and the music is the chatter-tap
of autumn branches,
the cackle of restless crows.

When I reach the fence
the birds yawp louder,
yet my magpie-raven-rook
proves to be nothing more
than the tattered shreds of a bin liner
ravelled in the wire.

Relief is short-lived,
tainted by this lost chance
of reparation for the tiny bird,
and so it remains in my head
as blind-bright as before,
a smudge of fluff at the roadside,
its mate still flying on alone.

Cows

I follow the rutted path,
my boots snapping ice
as brittle as spun sugar.

When I reach the five bar gate
the cows emerge from the mist,
black-faced and liquid-eyed.

They shuffle from hoof to hoof,
paw the frost-hard earth,
and watch me, silent,
their breath hanging in the cold air.

Later, in the fug of the cafe,
I remember their velvet muzzles
as I watch the steam rise from coffee
as dark as their flanks.

On Hearing Gerry Rafferty's Baker Street

We explored each other, inch by inch,
in a guesthouse off the Edgware Road,
discovered London kiss by kiss,
made it ours, and ours alone.

I thought I'd dress like Annie Hall,
write novels and smoke Sobranie Blues,
you'd paint our Hampstead floorboards white,
read poetry in the afternoons.

Yet when my time for London came,
there was no you, no teenage dream,
all that was left was the drab routine
and the long commute on the Northern line.

And each time I hear Baker Street,
I recall that summer, way back when
we both believed the stars were ours,
so sure we'd make it to the end.

Wondering How Your Boys Turned Out

A love song was playing
as we left the bar,
and its three-chord promise
followed us outside.

I unfastened my jeans in the alley,
all fumble and beer-malt breath,
the brickwork cold against my back,
and we told ourselves it was passion not sleaze,
because it was us
and we were special.

Then you said you couldn't leave her
until your boys were grown
and I pretended to understand,
sang the song under my breath,
whispered the words
into your ear in the taxi home.

They still play it sometimes on the radio,
and I hum the tune,
wondering how your boys turned out.
Yet I doubt you'd remember the song
if you even think of me at all.

Back then we were still kids ourselves,
thinking we had no time left
when it turned out we had it all.

The Light

They showed me other countries,
always talking of the light,
and I still recall flashes of fuchsia
and dozing, shuttered villas
glimpsed from windows on the morning train.

My mother, slim and tan in her cartwheel hat,
would read aloud to us from the guidebook,
suggesting the basilica, the teatro, the frescoes,
and my father would call a halt for beer
in the shade of the colonnade.
We'd wander across the piazza,
urge shopkeepers to spread out
silver bangles and Murano beads,
unfurl silk scarves that billowed like parachutes,
only for my mother to shake her head.

And now, in the park,
I remember petals fluttering into the villa pool,
cupping half-drowned insects in my hands
and watching them rest
a few moments in the sun
before flying away on luminous wings.

I see a woman in a hat like my mother's,
swinging the lead of an unseen dog,
and think to myself, that if she were here
we'd talk of the light,
of the gold-green light of an English afternoon.

Violet Cream

At lunchtime I buy violet creams,
your favourite kind in the turquoise box.
We eat them in silence,
our old plaid picnic rug draped across your bed,
and I sit at your side in denial,
still sewing name tags
into clothes you'll never wear again.

I feel the rough blanket against my hand,
remember it spread out on summer Sundays,
long grass tickling my toes
and the chipped china plates stacked
with slices of buttered bread,
a quarter of thick ham,
your over-boiled eggs, yolks rimmed with grey,
and a single tomato for each of us
that tasted of sunlight trapped beneath glass.

Then afterwards, the violet creams.
'Perfect,' you'd say,
and my father would place his hand over yours.

I carry on sewing name tags
like you used to do for me,
some insistent alarm ringing along the corridor,
wishing we could sit on that rug in the meadow,
bat away wasps, drink weak orange squash,
just one more time.

You whisper something,
your words so fragile they hardly disturb the air,
and I press another chocolate gently against your lips
to hold the memory there,
as though to seal your departure
with this final perfect thing.